THE WELL-TEMPERED TANTRUM

The Well-Tempered Tantrum

John Talbot

David Robert Books

© 2004 by John Talbot

Published by David Robert Books
P.O. Box 541106
Cincinnati, OH 45254-1106

Typeset in Classical Garamond by WordTech Communications LLC, Cincinnati, OH

ISBN: 1932339396
LCCN: 2003115785

Poetry Editor: Kevin Walzer
Business Editor: Lori Jareo

Visit us on the web at www.davidrobertbooks.com

Acknowledgments

Some of the poems in this collection have appeared in the following periodicals:

Poetry
"Kindling" (as "Shavings")
"Late Manner" (as "It Was Over")

The Yale Review
"Eight Horatian Odes for the Fourth of July"
"E.S.L."
"The Song-Book of Justus and Merci"

The Southern Review
"El-Ephant"

The Iowa Review
"Nineteen Sixty-Three"

Quarterly West
"The Gardener's Address"

Arion: A Journal of Classics and the Humanities
"The Secret Accretions"

The Formalist
"The Maestros" (as "The Masters")
"New Year's Eve Poem"

Light
"The American School"

Grolier Annual
"The House You Were Born In"
"The Leaven of English"

For various kinds of help, the author thanks George Core, D. S. Carne-Ross, Joseph Parisi, Christopher Ricks, Mary Jo Salter, Jon Silkin (posthumously), Rosanna Warren, and the staffs of the Boston Atheneum and the Boston Public Library.

Contents

I. A Braided Aubade
Kindling 11
Chapters from a War Story 12
The House You Were Born In 14
Ten Subjects from the Last Summer in the Old House 16
"Is This Now Mine Own Countree," 17
Circuit Court 18
El-Ephant 19
Nineteen Sixty-Three 20
First Freeze 21
The Leaven of English 22
A Braided Aubade 23

II. A Classical Temper
Four Roman Odes 27
   i. The Consolation of Philology 27
   ii. Carta Postale 29
   iii. A Philological Crux 31
   iv. The Secret Accretions 32
The Song-Book of Justus and Merci 34
   i. Epithalamion 34
   ii. Merci Before the Temple 35
   iii. He Would Chasten Her 36
   iv. Her Love-Quarrel with Him 37
   v. On His Blindness 38
   vi. Night-piece 39
Three Hymns for the Day of Your Birth 40
The School of Mastery 43
   i. The Master Class 43
   ii. The Maestros 44
   iii. The American School 45
   iv. E.S.L. 48
   v. The Gardener's Address 50
   vi. Cardinal Newman Addresses His Books 52

    vii. To Professor Christopher Ricks, on the Publication of His Book
        on Literary Allusions 53
    ix. Palinode 55
Silvae, or Lumbering 56
    i. The Origin of Our Children 56
    ii. Foiled Grudge at Gloucester 57
    iii. Leavetaking 58
    iv. "That Creepeth Vpon the Earth" 59
    v. West Point 60
Eight Horatian Odes for the Fourth of July 66
    i. The Great Seal 66
    ii. The Fruits of Independence 68
    iii. "George Washington Slept Here," 69
    iv. Inheritance 72
    v. The Founding Mothers 73
    vi. A Parting of Ways 75
    vii. Uninheritance 76
    viii. The Pacific Theatre 77

III. The Gentlemen Tipped Their Hats

An End to Sorrow 81
Anniversary in Greece: Confined to Our Hotel by a Sudden
    Windstorm 82
Reconciliation to a Line out of Yeats 83
Fortune Cookies 84
Information Age 86
Trunk 87
Oncology Ward 88
New Year's Eve Poem 89
Late Manner 90

I. A Braided Aubade

KINDLING

You gone, I thought to look
for warmth in the pith of trees,
so I went to the chopping-block,
brought axe's edge to kiss
soft, knotty-hearted pine
whose sinews might warm mine.

Matchstick's rasp, blue chuff:
the fine-shaved kindling caught,
curled into twenty fists
that cupped their fingers shut,
till fire fastened to the wood
and wooed it close and hot,
and soon the room was warm enough
but I was not.

Chapters from a War Story

§ Fat apples draw the bow; burnt autumn releases
its shiver of darts. Never too far away,
never far away enough, the bruise of war
smudges her thoughts; somewhere in the house
there is a locket in a cedar box, she will find it;
gauze curtains ride the bell-cusp of a breeze;
deep tongues of wind; she is drawn to the window;
orchards are rocking the rocking that brings no sleep.

§ There are sunny intervals; there is chuckling like water
in braided brooks; unease—for now—has lifted
like the grass poking through. Words come through, too:
buss for what the light does to her cheek; *reticulation*
for that net of glare and shadow in the grove;
interstices for her thousand overs and unders.
Shuttles hum in the warp; prose pulls itself snug.

§ To seize the city: funny, he thought, it should bring,
from the other side of the world to these baking alleys,
whiffs of Freshman Lit: *The man of myriad cunning
ways, after he sacked the high citadel
of Troy*, and all that. Still, glares from natives stung;
doors had to be broken down, and one of these
was a library; he thought of her. So, later, to take out
her book, to savor words in his conquering language,
meant both homecoming and invasion. There were pressings—
petals, a lock of hair—but the hard thing
was the inscription, each letter's curlicue and fluke.

§ Chapters in staccato succession: events press in:
impossible to forget him, yet he must go

half-forgotten. Rotation of Easters and Christmases,
those are the only time-markers. One minor character—
at first just a man in his usual seat on the train,
seen mostly from behind and mentioned only
for being well-tailored—now has got a name,
a pedigree, pressing his claims as the phone
rings with news about her ailing mother.
Suspended banality of transcontinental flight;
hard citrus shafts of sun, Californian light,
not felt in earlier chapters; arrangements; home,
whereupon she discovers, heaped on the icy doorstep,
an ossuary of unopened newspapers.

§ Ply comes unwoven; sentences shamble, drift.
Whole chapters surrendered to interiors and mulling.
Less and less she dwells on here, more otherwhere.
Nothing fanatical: the weekly wash
gets done, that sort of thing. But just unclasping
the clothespins now can bring a transport: touch
of imminent release. She hears the light
on the back of summer leaves. When conifers toss
of a windy night, her dreams will sleepwalk out
to taste that shuddering. The well-tailored man
dropped out long ago; what was his name?
 —And her soldier, I assume she has brought herself
to think him dead. Yes, she is empty,
but has never felt so essential. I am afraid
to turn the page. Joy will be hard for her
when he steps in the door and lays his hat
on the cedar box, which he carved for her himself
before they were married, before the story began.

The House You Were Born In

Ignore the iron gate, the men at the door.
See how they let you pass?
This is, after all, your old house.

So slacken your pace,
Let a perfect stranger guide you through
These rooms, disarranged

In your mind like the paths of scattered leaves.
Nothing is changed.
Your ancestors still colonnade the hall

Where the wind rushes through the windows
And the rocking curtains
Applaud you as you pass.

The owls that nested in the dome
The night you were born
Turn hourglasses over the chance of mice.

In the conservatory, where childhood's daylight ebbed,
Your mother's metronome halves and quarters
Whole passages of time,

And celebrates the sequences of rooms:
From midwife's quarters, forceps
Still in her embroidered bag,

To cellars where furnaces
Greet you like kettle-drums.
Locked closet-doors spring open at your touch,

And in the study your father's safe
Confesses its combination.
If, having come so far, you should find

You lack the strength to open it,
You need not claim you feared, but forgot:
Forgot you were brought up to be

Almost a god,
Like the gods in the attic
Of the house you have lost.

Ten Subjects from the Last Summer in the Old House

Sepia: stiff-collared ancestors blink
Through tawny clouds of cuttlefish ink.

Persian carpet: the Moorish infidel,
Subjugated by Mother and taught to heel.

Snapdragons: how were those feral lips
Demoted to puppets on her fingertips?

Mantel: an altar, from which would stare
Father, long lost into everywhere.

Grandfather clock: in the hall one night,
Shock of a coffin propped upright.

Tempus Fugit stenciled into the dial.
The moon with her grimace. The sun's pursed smile.

Cancer cells: businessmen, canny and cold:
Bought low from her young, sold high to her old.

Presages nightly: news beyond speech
From lips I swore I could almost touch.

"Is This Now Mine Own Countree,"

       where the sea stops shaking its fists,
where clouds lounge, sated tabbies, in the window-seat
           listening to the late sun
           whisper its lists and lists
of euphemisms for *hissing fat* and *indigent heat*,
       and the rapids refuse to run?

       Where the sulking diadem waits for the queenly brow
and the crown jewels turn to shells in the beachcomber's bag,
           and the palace chaplain
           dozes in his pew,
untouched by the sunbeams that lark in the rafters and brag
       of the tricks they will play on his vision?

       Where the brass bell's clapper, carpeted in moss,
summons the summer brides from those nunneries
           whose pink swaying coral
           prays and ponders and prays
for submarine gales to flash through the arteries
       of this pranked and slumbering girl?

Circuit Court

Surely something beyond just pleasure
Drives them round it, goads his flesh, her
Rippling trunk. Even I help measure

The circuit: three hundred sixty-five paces.
I know I witness in their writhing faces
A mirror of my own; I know this race is

Endless; yet each lap kindles my resolve.
Feet of mine, pampered with insoles and salve
Nevertheless keep suing for relief,

Burn like expired archives of autumn leaves.
By just such tokens, some runners swear they arrive
At a longed-for threshold, which, they believe,

Hurdles the track like a coffered marble vault.
I believe in it, too: portal less seen than felt,
Ushering flesh and pleasure into court.

El-Ephant

"I represent the elephant," mouths his trunk,
Which has lassoed out to greet you, and before
You can manage a word, that rubbery hose has filched
Your bag of peanuts. "I'll see to it, of course,
That *he* gets these," and coils back into the maw.
No help from that pair of housewives on the roof,
Beating the dust out of the broad throw-rugs
Of elephant ears; nor from below, where four stumpy
Umbrella-stands divot the mud. Those flickering
Sequins that stud the creased and serrated prairie
Of elephant's flank, the scavenging parasite flies,
Broadcast high-pitched contempt for the indifference
Of the management towards its oppressed dependents.
Behemoth expanse later narrows, all at once
To a shoelace, a rip-cord, a heartstring-thick whip,
Cracking with mock-heroic petulance
At horseflies, stoutly ignorant of the bulk
To which it appends.
                    Where, then, among all these parts,
Where to look for El-Ephant, that wizened elder,
That dour four-footed buddah, that Ancient of Days,
Who stands with the patience and fixity of an oak,
Flesh scored with rivulets from the rain and wind,
Bearing up under the weight of his unforgetting eyes?

Nineteen Sixty-Three

Frost Who remain must choose: will they unfold those hot,
    Those molten flags that lick us from inside?
    Blaze brief like you, and imitate the honed
    Epigram's barb, the brandished reprimand,
    Clip of the catalectic foot, mid-stride,
    The fine, sky-searing punch of the space-shot?
Kennedy Let them stake ground like yours: to be holt-
    And pasture-shrouded, winter-blaze attended;
    To link limp iambs, make them rise suspended
    Like virtuous cobras that jockey and recoil;
    To measure, in their stride, New Hampshire soil
    And care to see October's yield amassed;
    To take their counsel from the thunderbolt,
    Leave foolscap seared with signatures of frost.

First Freeze

Pratt's Mill Pond, Sudbury, Massachusetts

When shirts stick to burnt backs, our family totes
Summer's beachbag burden to a pond Thoreau
Deemed "earth's eye." In its winking undertow
We bob like happy unplucked beams and motes.

By October, Walden casts a cold eye, but feels
The touch of stern Concord elders, who limp or crawl
Down to the shore like snails, ooze through the marl,
And lasso through the shoals like ropy eels.

But our winter pond is in Sudbury. We wait
For the plate tectonics of the year's first freeze
To fuse shore to surface, as if to authorize
The opening of the pond for the first skate.

But before we lace up, some willing soul must try
The thickness of the ice. It may *look* hard,
Until the boot's pressure breaks a huge toothed shard
Exposing the pregnant black to the innocent eye.

That yearly burden falls to old Munson Powers,
Who stakes his body as the whole town's token
To see if the ice will hold, or will be broken.
He lugs his two thick boys in tow, but lowers

A tollgate arm to halt them at the brink.
Refusing a life preserver or rope to grab,
He kneels on the ice, inches, elbows like a crab,
And—one more year, at least—he does not sink.

The Leaven of English

(1) Yeast, whose enterprise
Leavened the Thames Valley,
Made the South Downs rise,
And loaved the hills of Surrey;

And (2) iron, lots of it, fresh-scraped
From dark Sheffield mines, its filings
Sifted out double and double-heaped
By rodent-eyed Midlands hirelings...

All right, then, add a little
(3) Tuscan honey, if you must,
Some half-clad goddess's spittle
Lest the mixture dry to dust;

But mind you, let a New Englander—
Some stern descendant of good
Governor Winthrop or Anne Bradstreet, stir
The stuff, and make it fit food,

Wanting neither pomp nor pith,
Tongue-tripping, *begetting a temperance that may
give it smoothness*, though seasoned with
The (4) brine of Botany Bay.

From the leaf that grew in Cape Town,
Kingston or Delhi, grind a (5) spice,
Wherewith sprinkle. Clamp the lid down.
Let the years pass. Watch it rise.

A Braided Aubade

Earth's brink, while we two slept
    had dark and driftily crept
towards a jagged line
    where sea and cusping sun
honored their daily tryst
    and hotly, coldly, kissed.

II. A Classical Temper

Four Roman Odes

i. The Consolation of Philology

Come to console me, Romans? Such great *pals*,
the lot of you, who swear big-talking vows
to go with me—I quote your words—"as far
as far-flung Bombay's breaker-beaten shore;
whether you press beyond the Caspian Sea,
silk-strewn and leisure-loving Araby,
or where the Parthians wield the fluted shaft;
thence to the shores whereon Nile's deltas heft
all Egypt's dazzling mineral sediment.
We'll stick by you, compadre, if you're bent
on steeper grades: to tread the Alps' high spine,
beyond whose precipices spreads the scene
of conquering Caesar's best-selling *Gallic Wars*,
and with you bide the Rhine's meandering course,
crossing the sea to Britain's chalky bank,
Caesar's limit and the earth's own brink.
Ours is the power, in biting circumstance
to speak peace to the souls of suffering friends."
Speak, can you? Fine. Ask the lady, real nice,
whose heart she winches in her cordial vice,
squeezing it sapless, leaving it blue and bashed
along with the dozen others therein lodged.
Ask her what's left but words for the fool who looks
for consolation in battered Latin books.
And this little query, pithy and concise:
how long till she orchestrates her next reprise
that brings her all mock-penitent back here—
as if she thought some tactic of repair,

when the passing plough, beneath the garden walls,
grazes a rose too fragile for the shock,
could graft the blossom to the severed stalk
                                    after it falls.

ii. Carta Postale

"Dear Dr. Talbot:
                    Thought I'd drop a quick note.
Today we saw the Palazzo Pubblico
Where Dante was sent to mediate
A dispute between rival princes. It's so

Thrilling to think I stood where *he* stood!
The frescoes are Florentine and Sienese.
Wish I'd bucked down at Latin, and could read
The legends on the walls and tapestries.

Take care." Signed: former Latin pupil.
There you have it: the Dante she chose to admire
Is the politic one: not poems but people.
Poetic stroke of hers, to pare

Virtue down to an epigram,
Postcard's compass, trim its edges
To deliver its deft incision: *for shame,*
Dr. Talbot, that some battered text is

The paragon of your affections.
How long will you separate life and work,
Pull the two apart into tidy sections
Like some pricy Caribbean fruit? If I shirked

Declensions and conjugations, if I can't,
From these pedestals, eke out so much as one word,
It's a sluggard's shadow monument
To the human society I preferred.

How long since you looked up from scrawls on rocks
To return the frank gaze of a human face?
Our hearts are ticking like booby-trapped clocks.
Which will it be, Dr. Talbot: Romans or us?

iii. A Philological Crux

Loathe her, love her: while scholars wrangle *why*,
    I'm wracked between *caress* and *crucify*.

iv. The Secret Accretions

Ice, like the shimmering robe that blond blonde lets drop
        To her ankles, slips from the field,
And lets the brook break, chuckling, from its grip.
        She can't be twenty years old,

She and her friends, sunbathing girls, who go
        Dressed in their daring skin,
Parading everlasting youth—or so
        They'd have you think. Think again:

Think of how, six months hence, the last sour breath
        Of moribund summer's breeze
Will fail, and autumn pummel the grass beneath
        Carpets of frost-gilded leaves.

Outside, the seasons mend such damages,
        But not so the weather within:
No springtime thaws your limbs, no sun assuages
        Once winter gets under your skin.

Onto the very plot on which you'll drop
        Your ancestors fell first,
Who yearned for deathless things and tendered hope
        And now are shades and dust.

Join them tomorrow? Next month? Who can tell?
        Best live today with flair.
The secret accretions of a life led well
        Elude the grasping heir.

But learn good judgment now—for all your wit
        And pedigree won't budge
When men speak of you in the preterite
        And you become the judged.

Stern X, for all his piety, still died,
        Nor will ice soon release
Y to her pleading Z, who tried
        To rescue her. She stays.

The Song-Book of Justus and Merci

i. Epithalamion

Justus:
I want to bend the full hard sun
Into marbled alleys and flesh-plush holes,
Exposing tenured worms and tailored frauds.

Merci:
I want to sit with them in their prison cells,
Excavate, under the thin bruised foil of skin,
Barnacle-crusted, beating hearts of gods.

Both:
Love, grant us both and neither. Who can sing
Our wedding hymn, who can forge our ring,
Lives beyond words and rhymes with everything.

ii. Merci Before the Temple

Justus, I love your classical facade:
Windowless. Massy. Schooled and fluted stone.
Look, here's the plinth where Caesar was assailed,
And iron took the measure of the man.
Into the smoky narthex, to the block
Where long-haired Charles lay down his comely neck.
Altarwise, pull the iron curtain back
To find Ceausescu pinioned to the stake.

Grander: these myriad niches, where daily hurts
And negligences of each commoner
Are force-fed to them now, their just desserts—
Yet how, from beds of marble, all will stir
When Merci airs her humors in these courts,
Tatters the veil from rafters to the floor.

iii. He Would Chasten Her

Merci, before you minister
      The healing pill
To louts who are their own virus, grieve
For the innocents those louts you save
      In turn will kill.

Green once myself, I scoffed at horses,
      Rode "but steeds,"
Ranging from town to town, to rain
Pardon like minted kingdom coin
      On guilty heads.

Abetting the enemy—that was the term
      In a sterner day
For stinting on timely reprimands
Of sluggards who will not use their hands
      Or make their way.

Merci, provide: don't spread yourself too thin.
      The careless exact
Flesh from the spot where the heart must pound.
Just where you feel your heart expand,
      You must contract.

iv. Her Love-Quarrel with Him

"Not a woman merely, dearest, not"—
this was your language once—"not just a bride,
but a blessed deliverer," you said, "and I
love you not as man wants woman but
as a suppliant brings before the deity
his pledge of flesh and blood."

You said. Now I see through you,
want you the more, but see now
        a diminished thing,
          a soured something.

"Pity," you yawn.
 Pity, is it, indeed,
that your lacerations should only goad
my blunter cravings? That mere passion rushes in
to fill the hole where kindness once had been?

v. On His Blindness

Read to me, Merci. What I had long foreseen —
creeping darkness—has done better than creep. Now
          my toadies await rehearsal of
      the noble victim's pieties: *How soon hath time,*

the subtle thief of youth, spent my brief
light, etc., and would rather have it thus
          than see me restored and themselves forfeit
      franchise of their dear figures out of rhetoric.

"Impartiality," they'll croon, "made manifest in your very
person," nor will they see me stumbling in the temple
          their own hands reared to me. So read,
      Merci; I will have my dear

federal preacher, Ecclesiastes, with his silver cord and
teeming grasshoppers; I will have old frank
          Horace to anchor me from flight;
      Machiavelli never jumping in his groove...

but where are they, those astringent voices? I hear
their words, but where is the crack of the whip?
                              —How their old
          spirits warm to you, Merci, and surround you!
      Not till I heard them in your voice

did they visit my ears in love.

vi. Night-piece

There now, my husband, lay your head
      On Merci's breast. Though old,
Let rocking unweary the years away
      And leave you again a child.

Murdered and murderer, starlet and serf
      Have all gone down to their dreams.
The grandsons' grandsires list in the tar,
      But I remember their names.

Their moments, their flashes, are frozen deep.
      The black earth hides her seeds;
The scythe waits, hung in the loft, to let
      The grass grow up with the weeds—

Weeds so musky, rank, and sharp,
      If you felt their venom drop,
You would run riot with iron and fire,
      And that is why you must sleep.

Yours is to sever; mine, restore.
      Under a waxing moon
All that Justus has scattered by day
      Merci will gather in.

THREE HYMNS FOR THE DAY OF YOUR BIRTH

i

The day that picked you and marked you ever mine
Gave some shaft of its light to be gathered down
Into utterly other light, all black; you went down
Too fast almost, the light followed you down; love's
Stamina leaned into its burden, into age, pressing
Into the hard place appointed for the diamond.

ii

In one corner of pain
we hung a mirror
in a cherry frame

through which we looked out
on a passage tight
as a winter throat

We knew that brink
from a yellowing snapshot
sealed in a trunk
Think you said Think

I said and remembered
that quick offering
of hands and heartstring
when all was delivered

iii

Out bounced tears like beach balls.
Blue whales tumbled from bi-planes.
The octopus bruised her elbows.
The jellyfish prayed for spines.
In an instant, the collapsing sea
Shunted Jonah from Joppa to Tarshish.
It was then that we heard your cry.
Hands reached out to us like starfish.

The School of Mastery

i. The Master Class

Hurtful music. Yes, I love it, but
wince beneath its justice. Semiquavers'
flagstaffs tilting in martial accord; *vox
inhumana* promising that above
my foundering could rise something true and plumb.
What torture, when the fingers along the flute
find their stops. Or when fretted chords relax
into freedom, and I feel it, smoldering
in what is shrewdly called the perfect pitch,
which knows its cadences and falls through them
into the garden of its innocence.

ii. The Maestros

They pace themselves: that music will subside,
They've learned, by ten. They let the cellos' drone
Embalm the evening in formaldehyde
And let their wives' hands occupy their own.

Up go the lights. A platoon of ushers stirs,
Salutes them as they ooze into the streets.
Each he arrests his she, each she her purse.
Mass settlements into hotel restaurant seats.

Over dessert, advances breed retorts:
"But wasn't Ozawa *wobbly* on Fauré?"
Few in life's fugue so roundly ply their parts—
Just as a smart performance will repay

Their waiter, who, acquainted with such wiles,
Harangues them with his repertoire of smiles.

iii. The American School

Homer, eyeless yet unblind,
Maledict the undisciplined.
Let thy plaster brow discover
Gout and palsy, tumor, fever.

Fix thy winedark gaze upon
The poets of New Albion,
On every rake with pen in hand
From Mistress *Bradstreet* to Mark *Strand*.

Pardon, if it please thee, those
Whose early verses read like prose,
Whose times demanded that a man
Should wield an axe before a pen.

And pardon *Whitman* on his shelf,
Who only knew to sing himself;
For what he lacked of prosody
He made up being good and grey.

Nor make the objects of thy rage
All poets of the Postwar Age:
Blame not E. *Pound*, who first began
The Transatlantic Poets Plan,

Nor owl-eyed *Eliot* (*nunc et semper*
British as a Fortnum's hamper);
From testy *Frost* avert your harm,
Whose wintry verses keep us warm.

But rather, aim thy vengeful word
Against the lot, all unprepared,
Of upstarts who, with nail and tooth,
Contend to wear the laurel wreath.

Dante, firmly hold the rein:
Halt *nel mezzo del cammin*
The North Beach boheme, wont to dress
In Hamlet-shirts and watercress;

To wake at noon, peruse the ads,
Cavort with Berkeley undergrads;
Whose every poem makes malaise
Of what his latest girlfriend says;

Whose genius (he insists) denies
The need for such formalities
As punctuation, adequate
Noun and verb and predicate.

Let long-forgotten *Caedmon* make
A case again for cadence's sake;
Come lisp in lilting numbers, *Pope,*
To bards whose scansion squanders hope.

Shakespeare, stand you forth and speak
Against *small Latin and less Greek;*
For thence you drew joy, grief, and gall
Like arrows from an arsenal.

Homer, when punishment is dealt,
Then let thy healing touch be felt:
Staunch up the sap that enervates
The Muse in these United States.

iv. E.S.L.

Constrained to play a teapot Prospero,
I conjure puny tempests of English speech:
Yet how, tonight, those billows seem to dwarf
My students: Cheiko, Fraülein Himmelshof,
And Antonio Fernandez, twisting tongues to bridge
The gulf between *konichi-wa* and hello,

A neighbor and *ein Nachbar, flor* and flower.
My xeroxed vocabulary lists rain down
Fresh oceans on them almost by the hour;
Joker and teacher's pet alike half-drown
In the swells and breakers they must live among,
And pine for the beaches of the mother tongue.

Cheiko cannot fathom that thoughtless tuck
Of the tongue behind the teeth: an ell.
Just let it roll, I coax her. *Try again:
Flower.* "Frower." *And what has wings?* "A prane."
Clamberers up our century's teetering Babel,
We'll sooner escape earth's orbit than forsake

Old words. One night in ninety-one, between
Monika Himmelshof's tenement and the whole
Of such hearsay as lay outside East Berlin
Rose a wall of dust where once had stood the wall.
She had moved her lips without speech, she'd have said.
She'd hung forty-two calendars in her head

But couldn't remember where they were.
Nose pressed to the window of a banking jet,
Westbound at last, she fancied she could hear

In the metal rasp of collapsing landing gear
The scrape of one last soldier's bayonet.
Below, like a silver coin dropped in slow water,

Berlin flickered and went black. So now I pester
That selfsame woman with verb forms—by command
Of her last and sternest despot, Noah Webster,
Whose tome, turned weapon, she's kept close at hand
Through barbed wire, gunpoint, point of knife,
And the trenches of English as a Second Life,

Where new words and old worlds eerily echo.
As today, at reading practice: Mother Goose,
Pooh and (to make the petting zoo complete)
Peter Rabbit. And, by some oversight,
A paperback, *Shakespeare's Immortal Plays.*
Before I can snatch it up, Antonio,

(Whose father, fleeing Castro, boatlift-bound
For Miami, was squall-beset and wrung
From his dinghy as from a sponge, and drowned)
Lights on a page from the master of our tongue,
Mouths the strange words without scorn or love:
"Full fathom," he sounds out, "full fathom five!"

v. *The Gardener's Address*

(Delivered to the fellows of the College of Botany)

First let me break a little rule of mine
And add a disclaimer to that gracious introduction.
My works are perhaps not as widely known as *that*,
Though I do regularly move among the great,
And from time to time will startle, will delight
You by casually mentioning one by his first name.
Yes, a battery of young anthologists like yourselves,
Clean-shaven and richly qualified, have sought
To link me with some so-called school or movement:
The Parallelists, the Generation of '68, or
The Expatriates (my sabbatical at Versailles).
But there have been others of you—who each morning seek
A shortcut across the Military Green, where cadets
Mirror the rank and file of my manicure—
For whom my work will have merged into your lives.
Because you've not lived as long or loved as wide,
I have spoken for you. And when I speak my best,
I make fresh cutting coincide with a summer shower.
Those who decry my theatrics (and many critics do)
Have never walked at midnight through the quad
(As you have, wrapped in some Peruvian girl's arms)
Where I have erected fragments of Portland stone,
Patterned after such Inca gardens as have survived,
And rows of capulí from the terraces above Cuzco,
The very flower Pizarro prized, and ordered
Planted in their myriads in the Plaza de Armas.
In such moments it will have struck you that mine
Is a life of certain and ceaseless revision:
Each successive week brings me back to the spot

Where I wrought my masterpiece, once and for all,
And where I must therefore pull it off again:
Tomorrow and tomorrow, gentlemen.

vi. Cardinal Newman Addresses His Books

*"Providence has delivered me of every worldly passion, save this one:
the desire to acquire books, new or old books of any kind,
whose charms I cannot persuade myself to resist."*
—Commentary on Horace

Lucky for you the word that was with God
Made me a weakling for your type. In some
Corner of Foyles you court me, starry-eyed,
Whispering: *Come with us. Let's go home.*
With banker's prudence, I repeat my vows.
Pauline decorum urges to abstain.
But how can your graces fail to arouse
As if a man of cloth were not a man?
"We believe that Jove is king in heaven
Because we hear his thunder peal": so thinks
Lax Horace, and I love him, though he's proven
Me just as prone to worship cheap effects.
Theology's a fortress, but for some
The flesh is —right, I'm coming. Take me home.

vii. To Professor Christopher Ricks, on the Publication of His Book on Literary Allusions

Now then, I will unclasp your book. Then now.
Quaint music, maybe, but I like the sound
drowned voices ferry up to remembered light.
What pranking in this bevy makes it quick-
conceiving both in praise and discontent,
half-familiar spirits of our Familiar
Quotations, lucky strikes to brand a *K*
onto our shrunken *now* and leave it knowing?
Not flip, this wrangling in the tickle points
of copybook headings and their tutelary
gods—who, easily affronted, make to plummet,
with over-meddling, back within the covers;
but in that well (half-understood yet fully
fathomed) freshly sound I'll drown my looks.

viii. Obituary Photo of a Former Classmate

At school, this self-same dazed, marmoreal stare
Stood for a kind of loveliness: his mind
Was a house superbly haunted, disrepair
Too elegant to mend. And me, the bland

Suburban tract-house. *You're talented,* he cloyed,
Turn your back on the herd! He'd scoff to see me now,
Stooping to tuck a toddler into bed,
Kneeling there till her tossings melt to slow,

Legato breathing. In intervals just this still—
Swallowed breath of concert halls—he used to set
Cheek aslant violin. The rococo curl

Of fingers that followed; their tumbling, fret to fret;
The diving bow; rapt gaze, opaque as pearl:
That *was* a kind of loveliness. And yet.

ix. Palinode

The great master's deathbed recanting of his life's work...
　　　　　　　　　　　　　　—Lives of Poets

Hymns, yes, if you must. But this much I require:
No mention of my Sunday afternoon
Hobby of turning verses. I gave pain
A gait and grandeur pain does not possess.
Now she will not desert me. *Come,* she says,
Permit your muse to strum her well-tuned liar.

Silvae, or Lumbering

i. The Origin of Our Children

"Here," we agreed, "are the polo shirts wanting
pressing, here the inarticulate pet dog
who needs to be walked, shoes for shining, and all lie
within our power; yet where is the joy
in power unshared?" So we said, "Let us make
likenesses to hear our commands and to know
the iron's resigned huff, the teasing extravagant
gambol of the tugging Maltese, that sense of forgiveness
as the fog lifts from the domes of our buffed wing-tips
and they shine." So we created them, sitting beside us now
in the cool of the day, and we know what it is
to be known.
                    On the horizon of our thoughts,
only this smudge of cloud: whether the word
that explains why our natures could not endure
mastery, but craved increase, is the word
we revealed to them—*love*—or some other word.

ii. Foiled Grudge at Gloucester

A grief was arranged. The twilight surf supplied,
With its rows of rococo curls, the crafted
Formality he required. He would turn the screws;
Those mussels sucking silence from the rocks,
That's the idea, he thought. But stray disjunctions
Punctured his atmosphere: strewn seaweed annoyed him, it was lewd
And comical. Too, the ballooning costumes of the last
Of Cape Ann's summer people. All this, though,
Charmed her, and just now the sky fine-tuned that shade—
A burnished violet—so often glimpsed behind
Their moments of joy. She reached for his hand, he saw
His hand reach back, and the tide was going out,
The clouds were rolling back past Halifax.

iii. Leavetaking

Good night to that katydid lankiness,
Good night to the sundials in the garden of family mottoes,
Good night to the hard winks, to the cantelevered
Smiles, to the magazines of yesteryear
Waiting in waiting rooms, goodnight
To simpering at sunrise and lamplit afterthoughts.

Good night, good night, now there is no more grieving
For the afternoon's thinning pate or midnight's thickening middle.
The seas keep trying to throw their arms
Round unembraceable beaches, the hills
Keep raising their questions, let them—moot to you

At duty's margin, duty done,
Upspiraling mote in the cataract canyon.

iv. "That Creepeth Vpon the Earth"

Where spade just turned the soil
        naked and moist, caught unawares
in the insent sunlight, the homeless snail,

lording his antlers in miniature
        mock-heroic insolence:
eyes of pin-prick aperture,

but wide enough for the genuine feral
        chill to slip through: such vehemence
in a Sunday garden! Thimble's dose of peril,

tonic to bring the observer
        to concede, within the lowly gift,
lordliness in the giver.

v. West Point

I

"MASS. TURNPIKE—POINTS WEST"
        the onramp sign
in Boston reads,
        as if Design
had sent us the directive
        we take it for,
my wife and I
        in our married car.
West—that wide word
        sets us to wonder
how quickly we commend us
        to everything East-coast,
yet feel none the wiser
        for hours in seminars,
piqued donnish titter
        at angling allusions
or tinkling revolutions
        of teaspoons in Earl Grey.

Not that we molder
        in Boston, but may hanker,
if not for Hector or Hrothgar,
        then some weapon-wielder
of more epic habits
        than Lodges or Cabots.
We long, at each bend,
        for the haggard, cock-sure
bandit packing contraband,
        crouched in some outcrop

more Badlands than Berkshire.

So strike the board:
        No more: Away
to West Point, the nearest sunset
        our car can cope
with riding into
        in one drive's day.
—Are we soft beyond hope?
        Even this protest,
jejune and wordy,
        exposes how prissy
we've grown: "Now and then,
        one wants get *dirty*,
doesn't one?"

II

                                                  It's a Chinese thought
                                                         we
                                                         know
                                          to   think

                that West
                    Point
          is   "west,"

    but
    here
    it
    butts
from our map's
    brink

                                westernmost
                                       as
                        one day's   pressed
                                drive

              is
      like   to
              link

   us
to scenes of fabled
    occident.

                                But isn't it
                                    an
                           acci   dent
                                of
                          point of view

      that
right's the ob-
    verse
of wrong, and left

                                        is other
                                          than
                                         right?

            Just because some
       east-   to-   west-
                    far-

ing
Magellan
should
neglect

                        conventional
                   terms of perspective, or
                           Mercator
                            project

                                        his own
                                        bearing on-
                                        to ever-
                                        yone's map—

—but just
    at   that
      spot
where these muddled

                     musings had left
                     us   con-
                      vinced the world

63

                                        's out of joint,
                                              we
                                           pull into
                                            West
                                            Point.

III

Below us on the military green
         the marching files of synchronized cadets
                  riot with the springing serpentine
                           twining of Chinese dragons sans bulbous heads.

"Average age," reports our tour guide,
"barely nineteen."

                        Indeed, that their marching looks like art
nearly effaces the fact that the bacchic
thyrsus on each boy's back is a gun,
that our artless hours of sleep-in Sundays
turn on their clockwork discipline.

Surprise, too, how quickly wanderlust
for lawless country about-faces
when the wandering find, not local color,
but hues of a planet's general choler.

So driving out of town, we stop,
fatigued in our fashion, at a roadside Wu Hong,
and issue our orders for take-out chow mein.
Boston-bound, we munch our way down
to a future ensconced in our fortune cookies.
The thinly-veiled threat

Enscrolled inside
is classic Chinese:

> *The more*
>   *you sweat*
> *in peace,*
>   *the less*
> *you bleed in war.*

We are full. Cadets' images retreat
into the Lethe of our rear-view mirror.

Eight Horatian Odes for the Fourth of July

i. The Great Seal

Beggar beseeches banker
Who without turning his head
Lets drop a dollar stamped
With an eye on a pyramid

Prospector squatting amidstream
Pans water through a sieve
Black bear hounds the bee swarm
And paws for gold in the hive

Farmer pages his almanac
Cruising clouds overhead
Ought to lie low as dishrags
Arch high as eyebrows instead

High in granite aeries
Hunter crouches prone
Fixes a buck in his bullseye
Wife lies abed alone

Under far porches of marble
Diplomats knit their brows
And there's boiling in the kettles
Of the Senate and the House

Senator lifts the receiver
Darling he says *I'll be late*
And the champing mint keeps striking
Fresh currency of state

Between the grey green oceans
The moon binds with her beams
The wife the farmer the beggar
Night will loosen their limbs

And now frost glazes the pepper
The conifer bows and sways
But an eye peering over a pyramid
Waking   watches   waits

ii. The Fruits of Independence

The grass was never as green as when
        the lemons began to fall,
fleshy and debonair, to the lawn
        of Independence Hall.

Grandly they beckon to be undressed
        to the plump wedged pith—not sweet,
but steeped in that bitterness only the blessed
        Have tasted. So let's eat.

iii. "George Washington Slept Here,"

crowed a plaque slapped square on that canopied
behemoth. So then, some dustbound float, some
           bed, expects to accrue such pilgrims
      as cairn themselves up before herms and altars?

Which caste of shutterbug gawkers doesn't include
me: no tourist, not given to reverencing
           "national heroes" (two words lately dimmer
      than the tarnished currency their namesakes mug from:

the first term, a label for that misplaced love
whose outlines come clear when outsiders are loathed;
           the second, a plaster residue
      from days before lean, untenured historians

uncovered, behind the alabaster jaws
and stiff-upper-lips in our Hall of Fame
           not the expected bitten bullet
      as often as moldering wooden dentures);

least of all, communion with crystals or bed-posts.
So what, then, in me managed to hear—
           still stranger if I myself supplied it—
      utterance from that lifeless lumber?

I would not call it speech, but formal pleading
poured into woodwork's volutes and scrolls.
           For which, if I could find human words,
      I might put down some like these: "Inmate

of your violet, late, and fatly underfed
century, set it down to more than yokel
          piety that brings these crowds to the site of—
   the word will make you cringe—veneration.

They come to pause where charity knew repose,
where limbs once numb from bracing a nation's
          lifethroes, where a gentlemanly mind,
   scored and almightily battered, found

some rest. And they leave with a glimpse
of rich prefigurement: George Washington
          dreaming. Against frost and blood, against toes
   coming off with their bandages, against

(it would not be too much to say) the potentates
of this low world, I, the handiwork
          of some nameless Middlesex joiner
   knew how to offer his heart the just gift:

respite—not severance—from gravity's pull;
hours unfelt, where, under eyes fast shut,
          horses, some cantering, others placid,
   freckle a stint of bluegrass upland

mounting to a many-windowed house, whose gauze
curtains themselves ride the bell-cusp of a breeze;
          beyond which, between land and sky, another
   banner: broad stripe of Potomac cobalt.

If, in that cell of a century you pace,
there remain time and will to restore to worn words
            something of former luster, consider
        hallowed: because George Washington slept here."

iv. Inheritance

General Washington (so he prefers to be called,
Even on this side; so the children passing by
Now call him in all affection) is among
The tenderest we have ever had. Just arrived,
Swimming as he was in that wash of disenburthenment
In which lightheadedness precedes invigoration,
He said in his thoughts (though he did not speak the words):
"Now, perhaps, I'll be able to change these teeth
For a new set," and he blushed to see
That I had understood. I say it is that modesty
Now reins in the orbits of a hundred worlds
That turn around his star and call him Father.

v. The Founding Mothers

Not quite my cherished charity-cases:
they refuse to drop waylaid, roadside,
into my rescuing arms. Instead,
they beset me like horseflies,
      and coven their perplexities
      between pitched wingbeats. Not

proper villains, not Lady MacBeths
blessed with glamour and enterprise,
but visibly vexed. Unstaid.
Flickering neon flightpaths of irate
      yellowjackets,
      electrical wits,

but witless simply to fly out
screenless windows and doors.
Preferring the crowded semaphore
of public overture and cant.
      To which I'd apply blunt
      indifference, but can't

shake my stake in the canvas they work:
the mis-matched patch in the counterpane,
beggardly moons on dog-eared calendars.
Eyesores, but not so blighted by
      the spectacle of age
      to conceal the heritage

I trace to my own brawling nurseries
and late-night tossings. They do not need
rescue any more than I could give it,
but do press me with the fact that they are kin,
      my kindred, facts of the needy
      world they delivered me in.

vi. A Parting of Ways

Against my friend here, Ferris, who holds it kind
That every creature find his own kind of right,
        I would aver: Not so, no mastery
    Ever was forged in that cozy furnace.

Let every scientist find his own kind of truth,
You might as well say. Phoebe, your elegant wife,
        Herself a neurochemist, how she'd
    Shiver—and justly—with indignation.

But in the highest places, still no shivers,
But strange composure with our ribald princes,
        Whose English (now Uh-mare-uh-cun, now
    Oxbridge variety) baldly mingles

Known words with unused meanings. *William* goes
Colliding with *Jefferson*; semantic charge
        Now chars the synapses that fired once
    Chaste at the mention of pale *Diana*.

No mourning, but lying in state as not since
Domitian. Atonement? But *that cannot be,*
        Since I am still possess'd of th'effects
    Sinning procured. That was Claudius, not

Me, who used that gerund that so offends you,
[*Hamlet* written above]
Ferris. Leave, then; but your outrage cheers my heart:
        Some hope remains for you, for me, if
    Even *your* tolerance has its limits.

vii. Uninheritance

Welcome to the slough of our parents' disport,
American. They told us the stars are just gas;
      scaled the stilts of slogan to mock
            absolutes: <u>piously, absolutely</u>.

Freedom, they crooned, but their range could not compass
the other notes in the scale. They'd have freed
      earth from her patriarch, Gravity, if only
            chanting and shouting could cow the despot.

Shackles they did break, shackles we'll yearn for,
come to our instant of tetherless freefall,
      our eyes finally open, but not with the double
            horror of those who live on to witness.

They professed to love trees, but they hated roots,
and pulling up theirs they left us rootless,
      new race of the eracinated, free
            only to propagate others like us.

viii. The Pacific Theatre

How to withstand their gaze, these men whose names
Are sunken here? How, when we bubblingly lack
Their courage-chilled-to-marble, their brass-tack
Demeanor and I-beam posture? How to clasp hands
And nuzzle, while above our heads they plod:
"For *you*, TV-tepid progeny, we died?
You whelplings bask in the slackness we deplore:
A time of peace or anyway not of war;
Platoons of waiters whose only tour of service
Is whisking you couples every prissy plate you order.
The peace we bought you, you mistook for ease.
Sated now, aimless, you ramble along the border
Of our granite war memorial. And still later,
You'll loll at some show at the Pacific Theatre..."

Yes, the Pacific Theatre, whose marquee
Mingles, nightly, neon palms with neon sea;
From whose vaulted lobby a crystal chandelier,
Hung with flocks of faceted tear-drop gems,
Lures in the light and sends its shattered beams
Scudding like lucent bon-bons across walls and floor.
At intermission, ladles debonairly bob.
Bigshot and near-miss hazard their hob-nobbing
Prattle, and night after night their chatter hums
And trips with a pleasing tumble off the tongue
And cheery energy into the ear. At bottles'
Throats, a dozen hands; across threadbare
Mauve carpet, the scuttle of thrice three dozen feet.
There, by the fountain, a quartet of elbow patches,
A pair of pipes and beards, convene to fete
Their luck at being happy, hale, and here.

Mirrored lobby, lapis molding, potted palms:
Yes, they commemorate a lapse in fate
By which our well-born lot was born too late
For the last war, and just in time to make homes
For the toddling corps that will fight the next.
What then: must we pretend to feel vexed
At the pacific horrors of peace,
Try to jockey discomforts into martial agonies,
Suck dregs from the deep-drunk pleasure bought by those
Who fought for peace, not ease? No. Though our uniform
Fits an usher, not an officer, on it goes;
And we and ours will make our way in time
To some wider and less domestic theatre.
For now, keep holding my hand. Just tighter.

III. THE GENTLEMEN TIPPED THEIR HATS

An End to Sorrow

There now, my sorrow: evening's come, so hush.
We longed to feel this shroud of shadows spread
About our shoulders, velvety and plush,
Not knowing the embrace we coveted

Would seize and subdue us both. But I can bear
To shoulder the mantle of the insent light
When, soon, the doors of morning swing ajar.
You will not wear it so lightly. Already night

Has drunk her tart celebrity to the lees,
And the thunderclouds that packed the balconies
Are stirring and restless to go. Her last weak ray

Fretted through latticed elms, the pale moon drops,
And trailing her high sky-shrouding drapery,
Listen, dear, with what stealth the nighttime creeps.

Anniversary in Greece: Confined to Our Hotel by a Sudden Windstorm

Laurels racked in a gale   old story Apollo
Daphne after all these years   the shining
god bears down   she bends but will not
give
        those were hard hours aloft
brought us to this much-vaunted
paradise   wanting respite   only to sit
witness to these buffetings   I could be
glad   could you too be glad   once
again the prize goes to the slow
holding out
        winds slack   all still   the rest
is on the laurels

Reconciliation to a Line out of Yeats

She—when a slew of shrewd barbed hurts
I'd done her came, at last, to redound
to my own grief—she proffered not payment in kind,
but lips at my ear and whispered words:
      "Even," she shushed, "those platinum blonde
angels, who wear for skirts
'the dim and the dark cloths of heaven'
show, on occasion, some slip,"
      and then it was back to laughing, then
it was back to lip to lip.

Oh how you angels laugh. And how you weep.

Fortune Cookies

i
Overheard in the pew:
*Such abrasive love
In the original Hebrew!*

ii
From his lofty view
He takes in continents
None of which is true.

iii
Attending not to sense, but sound,
What I never sought, you found.

iv
Downcast, I found
Red shoots flowering
Low to the ground.

v
Among all the voices
I heard only echoes.
Where were their voices?
I only heard echoes
Among all the voices.

vi
My other, in the mirror, felt
The sting of self-importance when
I came, daily, to regard him.

vii
Overheard in the pews:
*Who could read the Bible
Out of such blue eyes?*

viii
Fit these lines to the oracle's measure? OK:
Your wake will converge like chopsticks on
Your fleeing boat; your milky contrails will lie
Like pick-up sticks above our heads; the cars
Will drip through their catheters; your goings
And comings will tell the truth about you.

ix
let us water that blossom let us bring
the vase to overflowing can we
drink like that cut stem

Information Age

From parroting that ours is the Information Age,
Some respite, please. Say that on crumbling piers
Fishermen wait; say the tossing wife pines
For footfall in the courtyard; report that the mountains
Are, and are, and are, underneath
Ice that was not, and is, and will not
Be. I can learn nothing from news.
Bring word of what I already know.
That breath is short. That daylight inches.
(These apples ripen to redness or paleness.)
That love comes shedding confetti from gnarled
Branches above; that canyons are deep
And from the deep canyons word sounds, resounds,
And will not alter and wants no age.

Trunk

"Virtuous cobra": so you might call this comical
Length of hose, if you felt the need to name it.
"Cobra" for its fleshy reach, for its hooded
Aperture, its drowsy insouciance while awake
And its wakefulness drowsing, coiled for the spring.
How, in the manner of a quiet, efficient nurse,
It senses need and at once attends to it.
I am barely aware of thirst before my trunk
Has lopped bright bulbous fruits off low-hanging boughs,
Loped them into halves and wrung the juice
Into my parched mouth. No sooner chafe
At the equatorial heat, than it reaches down
To dredge the stalled riverbed of its mud
And scoops up a cool mud-sluice behind my neck.
And when I must put on terror, ratify
The terms and boundaries of my dominion,
It raises a trump to make the blood run chill,
A clarion of mingled art and governance,
So like to, and in the end so much unlike,
Any of your artists or politicoes:
Wise as a serpent, harmless as a dove.

Oncology Ward

When the man Adam had quitted God,
"I'll turn," he said, "these lumps of sod,
And take the even with the odd."
But it had been for Eve (whose hand
Had never touched a plough) to find
A wide groomed plot and break new ground.

You and I, likewise yoked and sealed,
Came soon to the end of the row we tilled,
Our part in the telling all but told.
And not sowers only, but also seed;
So must the same bitter choice be made:
Whether you must follow or precede?

Pale apples ripening in the grove—
Pick one and offer it, daughter of Eve,
In the hour of your taking leave.

New Year's Eve Poem

We shall be spokesmen of the year's last word.
It should surprise us both, since it will be
      simple and unintended, hardly heard
      above the traffic of the falling snow;

ample enough, like old calendars, to contain
whole histories of our apt or inept gestures;
      yet, like the fall of a felt hat, remain
      almost elegant for its silence.

LATE MANNER

Something expired. At the turning
A spirit was gone. That which was
Turned to sepia: high collars, punting,
Waxed mustaches, parasols.

From bridges, children stared in the river
And felt themselves, also, halved.
Old manners were patently over.
New manners had not yet arrived.

The old, without waiting to speak
Their parting lines in the act,
Learned to exit the way of pipe-smoke.
Uttered nothing. Utter tact.

Steamy ghosts rose from the horses'
Maws as they champed at their bits.
The ladies reached for their purses.
The gentlemen tipped their hats.

John Talbot took his doctorate in Classics at Boston University, where he taught Latin and Greek in the Academy program for eight years before taking a post at Brigham Young University. He is the author of a number of articles on ancient languages and English literature.

Printed in the United States
57596LVS00008B/277-288